THE ETYMOLOGY OF SPRUCE

THE ETYMOLOGY OF SPRUCE

Poems by Joyce Wilson

ROCK VILLAGE
PUBLISHING

MIDDLEBOROUGH, MASSACHUSETTS

First Printing

Rock Village Publishing
41 Walnut Street
Middleborough MA 02346
(508) 946-4738

ACKNOWLEDGMENTS

These poems first appeared, some in slightly different form, in the following publications:

LITERARY MAGAZINES:
"Norwegian Spruce" in *Agni*; "Snow" in *America*; "Lines to Allegra" and "There Are Days I Cannot Read" in *Antigonish Review*; "Near the Beach, Shinnecock" in *Christian Science Monitor*; "Hymn" and "Provisions" in *Cyphers*; "Grammar Lesson" in *Denver Quarterly*; "The Advantages of Driving" and "Loosestrife" in *Descant*; "Allium" and "Collector of Guns" in *The Drunken Boat* at www.thedrunkenboat.com; "The Burning Man," "Spruce Down," "Woman in the Dunes," and "Woman at Market" in *Harvard Review*; "Uses for Wood" and "Franklin Park, Boston" in *Ibbetson Street*; "Jack-in-the-Pulpit" in *Off the Coast*; "The Simple Past" and "Sweet Pea" in *Pegasus*; "Spiders" in *Poetry and Audience*; "My Father's Dreams" in *Poetry Ireland*; "The Etymology of Spruce" in *Rhino*; "The School Bus" and "Family Seen through a View Finder" in *Sandscript*; "Crows" in *Salamander*; "Asylum" in *West Crook Review*.

ANTHOLOGIES:
"Persephone" in *Orpheus and Company, Contemporary Poems on Greek Mythology*; "Brooch," "Fences," "Spiders," and "Spruce Down" in *Anthology of South Shore Poets*.

PRIZE WINNERS:
"One Cow Stands Quietly" won the Daniel Varoujan Award from the New England Poetry Club, Cambridge, Massachusetts; "The Rodin Drawing" was runnerup in the Poetry Competition at *Stand Magazine*.

Some of these poems may be read online at www.poetryporch.com.

Further gratitude to Stratis Haviaras, who accepted "Spruce Down" for the first issue of *Harvard Review*, to Seamus Heaney for the inspiration of his work on the page and in the classroom, to Lloyd Schwartz for his encouragement of long poems, to Fred Marchant, K. E. Duffin, and Katherine Jackson for their objective critiques.

Special thanks to Ed and Yolanda Lodi for their special care with this manuscript.

For John and Kaelen
who share my search for the true sense of the word

Welcome to Nease Library's

Annual Poetry Night

April 13th, 2011

Featuring Poet Kate McCann

Magnetic Poetry Awards

Open Microphone

Original works of Poetry

Favorite poems recited

Please help yourself to refreshments

A special thank you to Linda Day and Friends
Of Nease Library for providing the refreshments

CONTENTS

II.

THE ETYMOLOGY OF SPRUCE

THE ETYMOLOGY OF SPRUCE

Spruce. Also Sprws, Sprwys,
Sprewse, Sprewsce, Sprusse,
Spruse, Sprus, Spruch…
Pruce, Prussia…Sprutia.
From *The Oxford English Dictionary*

Spruce: sprout, fermentation, country, tree.

Also *Sprws, Sprwys.* In the ground a single seed, then a tiered cone of consonants and vowels.

Sprewse, Sprewsce. A latticework of branches strewn beneath bright skies.

Sprusse. Night winds whisper of rivers and silk.

Spruse, Sprus, Spruch… A house, many houses, cobbled thoroughfares along an aqueduct,

Pruce, Prussia… hurrying footsteps running through the hard, rain-glistened streets—

Sprutia. On the edge of a field, the quiet revelry of a grove of fir trees.

I.

SPRUCE DOWN

The vertical form hewn
at the base to a point like a pencil
fell horizontal to rest on stiff legs
like a cannon in firing position
or like a giant centipede, rigor mortis,
the bark chitinous like a mollusk,
the sectioned log worth at least a cord,
kindling, mulch, compost.

With our talk we sorted through the refuse
the way the tree had once
sifted sunlight, playing,
dispersing the emptiness.

PERSEPHONE

The day I returned to my mother's world,
blue gentians bled magenta
from their dark hearts
like felicitous flares.

He had warned me that her land
would be dry as sandstone,
and in the days that followed,
I remembered

the crimson crescents in his eyes,
his knowledge of the night
and subterranean tides.
I pressed my lips to his brow.

The boat set out before daylight.
When the hammered shield of sky dispersed
and breathed like plush mother-of-pearl
and fed its azure color to the sea,

I turned to her:
my mother's skin had grown slack
and hung on her arms like cool silk
wrung loose from waiting.

Woman in the Dunes

Why would a woman build a house upon the sand,
knowing the parable of the fool?

Because she has seen the salmon color
of the dunes at dusk,
felt the invisible paths adjust
to her strenuous walking,
and understood the burden the earth
has taken on. The evidence
appears here more apparently
than anywhere else:
each row of hills is marked
by a thin black line
left by passing glaciers,
a stretch mark that unfurls
where the motion of the topsoil
gathers, hangs over, and falls.

Here the dunes *are* easily disturbed
despite the resemblance
of these billows of sand
to water. They
sag, roll, change proximity,
but nevertheless surround,
fill in empty spaces, and rock
those footloose objects of the world
to sleep, as if swirls
of protean grains are an architecture
of pores, and hills gigantic arms,
and on the surface of this
shifting body, we are held.

SWEET PEA

Young and giddy
tendrils like strings

of green spaghetti
groping

to hold your hand
the demure before-the-pods-come

companion
to an elderly loved one

who loves the pinky-purple
the scent of Venus's powder

the bonneted kitchen flower
caught

in a square vase.
While youth does not know its heart

the wise heart knows enough
not to stare

too hard
into the delicate

messy sprawl
that blushes easily

and needs cold weather.

HARDGATE

Snow was stealing into our world
in patches, assembling on
the larger surfaces before
he saw it falling through the air.

In this house she had shared her life
with her sisters. Her nieces came
often with their nephew John.
Now she lived alone. Today

the shuffling of the women
moving from cabinet to cupboard to slate
sink, the sharp clatter of the spoons,
the smell of bread quick fried in lard

all seemed unchanged and unchanging
since his last visit. Grey light fell
through windows sunk below the eaves
and ran across the coverlet

where Chrissie was confined in bed.
She barely heard the swinging door.
He knocked. She raised her eyes to greet
her grand-nephew, the visitor,

whose name was also John.
He walked into the room alone.
—When your family came to Glasgow
you were still a boy in school.

—And now married! And your father dead!
To think I would outlive them all!
She grasped his hand and squeezed it hard.
He warmed her fingers in his palm

until the snow began to blow.
It blurred the houses and the roads.
He went out through the wooden gate,
hard to open, hard to close.

SNOW

must be walked through,
felt on the skin, whether tuft
or filament, stitch or tear,
a sudden freshness
like anise on the tongue,

though the slightest
motions jostle and churn
like moths fluttering
against the curvature of sky
as beneath an inverted glass,

a nontranslucence,
the dappled flecks of a
pointillist's sleepy, mono-
chromatic dream, remnants
from another world

resting on boughs like rows
of herringbone, shags of chenille,
a quilt's new batting, or lacework
where threads were pulled
through and knotted,

holding light against dark
in a garment or field
glittering under the winter sun,
until the brilliant petals fold
and we feel the cold.

SOCIETY OF BOYS

The boy who lived on the hill walked
    until he could drive his parents' car.
I wrote his name in the haze on the bathroom mirror
    when I got out of the shower.

On our first date, he borrowed a convertible
    and parked near the local drive-in
where he offered to spike my ginger ale
    with Budweiser, Black Label, or sloe gin.

I wanted to believe him when he made a list
    of the virtues of his favorite drug.
When I heard him play the saxophone at dusk,
    I thought he was the boy I loved.

Seeing the name on the mirror, my father
    rubbed the color from his eyes.
He said nothing that day till we met at dinner,
    then proceeded to discuss the society of boys:

"Night is the time, and the theatre
    provides the only custom and ceremony
in a culture that thrives on turmoil;
    despite the crowds, you can admit you're lonely.

"Any downtown hotel would drown you in enough liquor
    to make the worst blather resemble serenade.
When you hear the night's obliterating laughter,
    order claret lemonade."

My Father's Dreams

When my father came home
he left his dreams outside

and brought in his failures
with toxic fumes of car exhaust

clinging to the shoulders
of his navy wool coat.

He hung his coat in the closet;
the vapors dissolved

into the summer air
above my mother's simmering casserole;

still he was unhappy
and sat at the head of the table

as if ready to divest
and crawl unburdened toward death.

He received our greetings like abuses;
they festered like a growing wound.

His disappointments cluttered up the house
like worn-out galoshes;

we tried to find a place for them
to get them out of the way.

Though it seemed we did not understand, we knew
outside, his dreams remained.

I saw their devastation and beauty the day
I opened the front door and stepped

over a skein of cobweb, discarded,
spangled in the rain.

THE RODIN DRAWING

The drawing hung above the head
of my parents' twin tufted-covered beds;

behind the glass, lying lengthways,
the figure of a man with one leg raised.

It was true, the head was far too black,
rendered solid with a heavy charcoal stick,

and the torso, not of any style or age,
floated, as if flung upon the page.

I remember needing to imitate its awkward pose;
on my back I lay, then one leg rose.

The story my mother often told portrayed
my father as a gallivant in New York, on his way

to his first paying job
when he spent the only cash he had

on a drawing, for the love of art
and some odd fascination with the work.

When we came to have the piece reframed
(years after my father died),

the restorer amused himself with our tale.
"A bookstore in New York, well, well, well.

Isn't this our lucky day."
He smiled at us in a knowing way,

took the paper carefully off the back,
lifted the pastel drawing from its rack,

held it upright, then upside down,
examined the paper and the ground.

Avoiding my mother's steel gray eyes,
he said to the woman at his side,

"By the way, what's for supper?"
Showed no concern when she didn't answer,

went on, a curly-headed judge:
"Possessions like this are like a marriage,

what looks like the real thing
turns out to be another failing

in the eye of the beholder;
you'd as soon have one as have another.

Now you're getting on enough in years
to know how often something real appears."

The fragile paper seemed the sole surviving part
of my father, his love of art.

I vowed to keep it
regardless of the final verdict.

The restorer hugged his hairy fist.
"You said your father bought this

for a song in a bookstore in New York?
Do you know how much a Rodin might be worth?

This is not a fake.
Darling, don't let the table shake!"

THE TAXI FROM TOWN

Early on, we were all aware of the taxi from town,
a yellow vehicle of escape idling in the woods.

My father was often doing what he wasn't supposed to do,
such as arriving in a taxi that nearly snagged
its low-hanging chassis on our rutted road,
driven by a man whose face registered horror
at our pastoral surroundings: daughters with uncut hair,
lawn with uncut grass, and all the neighborhood dogs
descending and howling at the strangeness
of the city vehicle and the invasion of privacy.
And I would have to forgive him for dying.

The idling yellow vehicle would remain in the woods,
recognizable, and the setting didn't change drastically,
except for our address—
from Glen Mills to Chadds Ford, as if it were suddenly
more important to cross the creek
than to grind corn on its banks,
as if nothing more was ever going to happen.
And I would have to forgive him for dying.

Our upbringing was the kind
only a Rousseau addict could provide,
and when we could barely talk at puberty,
we had to admit that the strategy was not working,
but it was too late to revert to lessons
in etiquette: the 'Sixties were upon us
and our spirits were converting to true energy.
We were nearly convinced that we might
be able to be children forever.
And I would have to forgive him for dying.

He showed little regard for chronology,
arriving at a local movie in time
to see the last scene first: the wound and the blood,
the boy's tears, and the hero riding off as if forever.
I suffered with the fear for years
before I saw the value of beginning with the end.
And I would have to forgive him for dying.

When my mother made the statement
about a famous movie star, rallying
to complete our moral instruction:
"I don't see why men find her so attractive,"
our father replied,
"Honey, did you ever look at her?"
Meanwhile, we slipped out the back door,
a new freedom found
in lipstick and high heeled shoes.
And I would have to forgive him for dying.

The taxi driver soon befriended our dogs.
He could be seen resting his back against the cab,
turning the large pages of the local paper
while they lay at his feet, nosing their flanks
and abdomens in the search for colonies of fleas.

As our father climbed into the back seat,
my mother looked frantically for his instructions.

We could hear the motor running,
then the hush of rain,
with that queasy feeling of being left behind
on a beautiful warm spring day.

HYMN

When my thumb was flattened
in the frame of our neighbor's swings,
my father examined the bubble of black
and blue under the rippled nail.
In a day or two, he said,
with all the authority
of his medical degree,
your thumb nail will fall off,
then grow back, a natural beauty.
But it grew deformed. Square
with a triangular moon. Ugly.

Was he as wrong again
as he was with me?
Never said the foxglove,
some the marguerite.

Exploring library stacks,
I remember his love of reading,
his refusal to be intimidated by the cover of a book;
his voyage around the world by steamer,
described in letters home to his parents;
his role in the war, when he asked to fight
on the front lines in Germany but
was sent instead to Puerto Rico,
where he diagnosed the president's
illness and won a place at the table
with the heads of state,
a most distinguished guest.

How much did it matter
that he missed the front lines?
Most said the cockscomb,
least the dandelion.

A research specialist,
prisoner of routine caught
in a series of 16 mm frames;
the mad scientist in torment
over the tally of deceased white mice;
the son of a minister,
hoe in hand, dancing in the corn;
the laborer weeding
the brick walk, pausing to rest,
the blood of exhaustion (really
ketchup) dribbling from his lips.

Has he seen his finest hour
as gone before or since?
Gone said the wolfsbane,
come the hyacinth.

He gave me perfume
that was too strong,
a recording of the latest Albee play
that I didn't understand,
a bicycle that I needed
years to grow into.
I hated his quiche lorraine
and could never read his favorite
book, *The Alexandria Quartet.*

Would he admire the woman
I have become?
No said the nightshade,
yes the geranium.

Uses for Wood

My grandparents lived next to a steam house
that forced yellow clouds through underground vents
to warm all the houses, like breath
from a municipal divinity.

After the Second World War, my parents shoveled coal
into a cast iron furnace coated with asbestos.
We called it the snow man. Pale and round,
he carried flames inside his belly.

When I was twelve, we converted to oil.
Out went the snow man and in came
the large tank which kept the liquid fuel
hidden, like unseen love.

The year of the oil embargo,
my husband and I explored the suburbs
until we found a wood-burning stove.
We stacked split wood in pillars and rows.

The columns of wood cast longer and longer shadows.
We warmed ourselves, preparing for the winter cold
with something we could hold.

Now, when the evening fires start,
I am drawn out of the darkness
to an old incendiary heart.

SPIDERS

I am plagued by the invisible ones,
the discarded silken lines
that raise
an irritating film on the forehead,

and I look up only
to find dusty tangled nests
at the ceiling's edge.
The shadows create impossible alphabets.

All morning I wait for the moment
my mind settles into the intricacy of webwork,
and the pencil circles and loops
without stopping.

PROVISIONS

Two are better than one...for if they fall, one will lift up his mate.
                                    Ecclesiastes 4: 9-10.

Our first car needs a push to start;
every evening we lie together on an old tarp
gazing up at a vast universe of engine.

Equipped with a month's provisions—
freeze-dried stew, your father's pup tent—
you vow to provide for me, and I for you.

When I voice dissatisfaction
with the contradictions of the world,
you study carpentry,

and when you are classified 1-A,
I make you a necklace of malachite,
a fitted leather vest.

Our honeymoon is a paradise in Maine
without heat or running water,
a boat with oars but no motor.

We resist the temptation of Canada,
stay in the city for the summer
and paint the back hall yellow.

At different times, our dreams emerge.
I capture fireflies in a jar.
You release a wasp into the wind.

While you are looking for a job,
I cut up onions for soup.
You bring a motorcycle home in cardboard boxes.

Suddenly I am homesick.
You vow to convince the landlord
not to sell the building.

How quickly you turn to me and say—
crank case oil on your shirt—
"You want to write? Oh. That's hard work."

WITH MY MOTHER AT THE MUSEUM OF FINE ARTS, BOSTON

The Open-Air Breakfast, by William Merritt Chase

In the painting, breakfast outside
begins at mid-morning. The back yard
has all the accessories of enclosure:
a Japanese screen to soften the brown fence,
a fringed hammock to rest in,
roses on vines the height of eight feet.
The children complete what the adults began,
voicing characters from the melodrama of their lives,
certain that to be silly is to share in the underside
of meaning, while the dog lies in the grass nearby
sleeping off the density of his dreams,
and the sunlight dispels the night's solemn umber;
the absence of roof invites
fluctuations of breezes and light.

I would paint a portrait of you, a widow
for seventeen years, at breakfast alone
on the flagstone terrace
under the bronze shade of the flowering privet,
before sunlit shafts break
over the roof of the gabled house
and you walk to the corner and take a bus
to your office in the city.
How composed you would look
in the emerging light of morning
where the uncut privet blooms.

Near the Beach, Shinnecock, by William Merritt Chase

*"An artist's summer vacation is his busiest, happiest time;
inspiration for the rest of the year."*

He paints with a frenzy to repeat
the ebullience of summer,
as if one can possess
the zenith of one season
and carry it into the next, can
open a household and fling the children
into a transient world of daylight
flickering on a sapphire sea,
on glossy grass-covered dunes,
on a child's face and hands, a woman's windblown dress;
where the shadows are vibrant
lavender, never gray or black;
where each grain of sunlight makes its own color,
its own dazzling swarm,
drawn through the threshold of winter.

Franklin Park, Boston, by Maurice Prendergast

Prendergast loved to paint the movement
and spirit of the public at leisure:
Dorchester, fin-de-siècle, is paradise
in which a park seems a garden

of light, shimmering, enclosed
where women carry parasols and walk
in the eddying flow of the promenade.
We relish this view of your parents' world.

Move, and the colors on the canvas move.
Squint, and the figures on the landscape change.
He did not depend on facial expressions
to communicate observations of character.

The bright parasols have become balloons,
the dresses colorful patterned shirts,
the promenade a soccer game
at Franklin Field where the Haitians play.

Because he left the features blank,
the artist showed more than he knew:
the future prefigured, your world in mine.
Pewter-colored thunderheads approach

like wind-driven smoke from festal flares,
announcing a shift in horizons.
Where paradise provides a luminous energy,
the garden is larger than the frame.

The Artist's Studio by Childe Hassam

The woman on the couch sorts unseen reams of solitude

An arm's reach from objects to paint and to paint with.

Light from the sea bears timbers of airborne motes

Toward the mahogany, a fertile red plain.

Behind the wainscot a mouse unwinds inches of silken fringe.

Masses of sketches, notes, false starts begin

The afternoon drift. He will not come.

Soon she will arise and turn to enter the adjacent world,

To play the part, moved but unmoveable.

With a sower's hand, the clock scatters time.

TRIPTYCH: ENGLISH AS A SECOND LANGUAGE

1. Grammar Lesson

"Qu'est-ce que c'est 'earthquake'?"
"C'est le tremblement de terre."

The textbook account of San Francisco
Is easier for them to accept than
The Caribbean fable of two secular men:

One gives life, one takes it away;
One has the persona of a patriarch,
The other a Faustian military man.

Then the print seems to shift on the page.
Space between the lines allows
For a silence that would undermine

The calm of the sunny afternoon.
I feel the sudden thud of thunder
Or a jet breaking through the sound barrier.

In the hard reflective surface
Of the textbook like a mirror, I
See them rising from the pit

Of their nation's recent history
Into the beveled skyway of the literate.

2. The Simple Past

In Haiti she learned the language
from a group of nuns
at the espaliered hermitage.

Impressed with the work she had done,
they made her a teacher
at the local kindergarten.

She came to the United States
and found employment folding clothes
on Dorchester's Washington Street

and every morning at the English class,
she studies the present tense,
the simple past.

"When I lived in Haiti I was
a teacher. Now
my job is laundress.

"My boss is Italian, hard on
women. He does not respect
the life of the Haitian."

She looks away and cries
caught between the state of being heard
and being heard unknown.

With vehemence she adds,
"When I have more money,
I give to the poor."

The others are embarrassed.
I would point out her mistake
and introduce the future forms

but today we must study
the present tense, the simple past.
They wield their pens and write.

Their essays float winged symbols
compressed between the lines,
waiting to be read.

3. Asylum

They savor proper names like passwords
and laugh at my homemade teacher's aids.
Watching their faces rapt in childlike trust,
I would never tell them I am underpaid.

They hope for better salaries, better jobs.
When I ask them for their history,
they voice a hasty monologue.
I recite quotations on democracy.

They reject my invitation to keep a diary.
"If I write what I think," one of them hoots,
"Duvalier will send his men out after me."
The others chant along with him, "Tonton Macoute!"

Mindful of what they need—
shelter from the city and approaching winter—
I tease them as they scowl at verbs,
the regular and irregular.

II.

FENCES

Newlywed
my parents bought a house in the country
where wooden fences marched

over hillsides
in bold punctuations of slats and posts.
The uprights wore caps like watchmen.

One year, I awoke
in the middle of a November night and knew
no one was paying attention.

There was a quarrel; our father
was leaving in his car. The next morning we saw
the leaning pole, the shredded wire;

the metal fence
of the empty sheep pasture gaped
as if all that was contained had burst.

I ached for a land ordered by fences,
as if happiness required
newborn lambs and pastoral ways.

My heart stood firm
clutching fast to old fears.
Now the landscape is growing strange,

and the fences sink
like brittle, arthritic bones
in an improvised, unmarked grave.

BROOCH

Persian Gulf, 1991

The oil-coated cormorant reminds us
of the likeness of birds to reptiles—
Its feathers glisten on its body like scales,

the narrow head protrudes naked
in the absence of a plumage crown,
the eyes are wild as if ready to strike

and yet all appears to be coated with gold
as if the front page photograph has captured
something precious and we might wear it on a pin.

The outrage in our breasts and throats is caught
on the surface, like a water bird
fighting to emerge from a gilt-edged lake.

ONE COW STANDS QUIETLY

Pervomayskaya, Russia. "One cow stands quietly, still alive,
with her stomach hanging out from a gash in her side."
AP Wire Service, 1996.

Her breath could still be warm.
Insert your hand in her side
and tell me of this war,

how all the horsemen came
with bullhorns and with leaflets,
kalashnikovs and boys

when I believed the truth
could be assessed and reassessed
in our four-chambered heart

of logic and of trust,
with humor and with grace,
before I understood

this regurgitated truth
comes back romantic pulp
without protagonist.

She can chew and re-chew
in quiet isolation
and self-communion.

As in the Dark Ages,
she will wait still for death
without imperative.

Tell me, what is worse
than blank imperative?
How can we leave her here?

I cough up phlegm, despair,
until revenge, or fear,
the impetus to act

turns bitterness to gall
and murder in my mouth
transformative and sweet.

Tell me of the strength
in the wise and feminine,
the stomach as a verb:

How much can we stomach?
Her organ is detached
and resting on the curb.

SKY MESSAGES

It seems that nature's envoys have withdrawn:
Pheasants traverse our path at breakneck speed
Rejecting our goodwill and outstretched hand.

Long-legged herons never come to shore.
On our approach, sparrows explode from trees.
A wedge of geese knits the horizon closed.

Even the starlings fill the skies as if to say
The seasons have run out of promises,
And we must learn to drop our guns and walk.

THE SCHOOL BUS
September 8, 1975

Now the police escort,
the crowds, the overturned cars,
the faces of the children
in the school bus windows:

I hear the epithets of hatred
spawned in the color yellow,
see the children caught
in the belly of a whale.

Once it seemed that whatever one needed
the other would provide
where the school bus drew a single thread
through the neighborhoods,

that the pumpkin color held
children of dissimilar parents together
where the Concord grape grows wild
beside the cultivated rose,

and the broad brick building,
once a school for the first grades,
houses its pupils now
that they've reached old age.

Once I saw the school bus
as a sunny place where children would be safe.
Then our history washed up over us.
Then we began to drown.

THE BURNING MAN

His mind refuses to die down;
it works at the top of its bent,
fueling locomotives' wheels.

Words curl and disappear
like fragile crimson leaves.
He has set his dreams on the horizon.

His rage is like cinders on the tongue.
Vision of an antichrist?
How he would laugh to be challenged thus!

How often have I tried to catch him
and douse the coals with all my passion.
But as I raise my voice and cry,

his mind increases and would engulf the house;
I want to run, except I know that
running makes the fire worse.

FLOWERING CHERRY

The flowering cherry stretched
its limbs like a young girl waking from sleep.
Blossoms festooned the delicate boughs.

We had just sold the house.
"Stay as you are," my mother said.
"Just be yourself, always."

At midsummer, we went back
to complete the transfer of ownership.
We could see the change in the cherry tree:

it had become someone else's idea
of the beautiful, a contrived idea
severed from its innate elegance

without the sensitive hand
that understood its secret,
the release of a graceful tracery.

I stood next to my mother,
a young widow with three teen-aged daughters,
and felt the agony of the vulnerable.

Then I understood how hard it is
to say to young tendrilled things:
"Stay just as you are."

CROWS

1.
The first one looks awry
with a single, crooked eye.

The next prefers to stand apart
preoccupied with self and art.

The third is just a slender form,
a fear within

that grows and gnaws and caws,
a withering.

2.
When I sat down to write,
I was free like a child,

but in truth I had a daughter
who talked back and cried.

The local grocery housed our meals
and memories

of the hurried step of my mother,
her worrying.

3.
I am beset by visitations:
three crows arrive at dawn,

alight on leafless boughs,
and guard their young.

They cannot sing but voice
a clamoring,

an unmelodious length of song
for daily bread.

THERE ARE DAYS I CANNOT READ
Poem with lines from Marianne Moore

Dürer would have seen a reason for living
in a town like this,
where across from the small movie theatre
a fine white church shares the block
      with an equally fine
stone library;

the owner's name engraved on the front
      is also the name of the side street
where automobiles stop for pedestrians
who cross quickly to and from the hospital
      emergency ward. Today I am one.
Not a frantic place

inside; the nurse at the desk
      remembers the name of each patient,
and the policeman on duty surveys
the waiting room with a seasoned sympathy, his gun
      a relaxed appendage for a rare
emergency. I must

go out in this New England climate of sun
      and wind and fog from the sea,
where homes are kept smart in a new coat of paint,
as if carefully controlled appearances held
      chaotic weather in its place.
I pass a woman

on the corner who picks up debris
        from the gutter and carries
a small plastic bag full of trash, housekeeping
gestures all intended to bring order
        to the small city square, impossible
of course

and the fine vision of the town, plotted
        over a hundred years ago
leads one from serious thoughts to melancholia,
a subject for Dürer later in life. Why? I don't know.
        I don't understand why Moore assigned
his name

to her poem about a prim New England scene.
        Nevertheless, *it is a privilege*
to see so much confusion, and I wish my feelings
were etched in limestone, rendered intricate and deep,
        but they're thin instead, and I have only
nausea because

I don't see art or symmetry or logic
        but people who are sad,
unsettled, worried for a loved one confined
behind the curtain; yes, *there is nothing*
        that ambition can buy or take
away. Today

I am waiting for news of a loved one's progress.
        I cannot meditate, only idle
through magazines and walk outside where
the ghostly white of the parish house and church
            proclaim *an elegance of which the source*
is not bravado,
            the no-nonsense
of vigilance.

FAMILY SEEN THROUGH A VIEW FINDER

1.
It is autumn. We walk through the leaves
that blow across the empty city sidewalk.
You say: "My brother was the one
whose promise matched his gifts
we never could enough admire."
Show the knot between your brows,
the catch in your jaw behind your smile.

2.
A Volkswagen at the front door.
Passengers scramble out, tumbling and laughing,
gasping and sighing, as if they had all arrived
together in the tiny car, joining ancestries
from Europe and the Middle East. Your brother holds
the car door open as they file into the house.

3.
It is crowded in the living room.
Your brother takes the golden sugar bowl
and passes it, polished like a lamp.
Panorama of the food on the table:
grape leaves rolled and stuffed, unleavened bread,
bitter greens, and honey rich with nuts.

4.
Another gathering, late afternoon.
It is spring, cold and gray.
All eyes turn toward the front door.
Your brother enters with a girlfriend.

We arc busy arranging chairs, opening
spaces, making room for them to sit.
He exchanges looks with your father,
who is doing poorly. Outside, snow
is beginning to fall.

5.
The empty room is dark. Slow illumination
on a steel blue coffin, center right.
Your father had already died in May.
We never thought your brother would follow.

6.
Long shot of the congregation in the New England chapel.
Pan across the back and zoom in on the women.
"He asked for the funeral."
"But a closed casket, and no wake?"
"He was so thin. From the tuberculosis."
"ARC," she said, correcting the other.
After a brief silence. "AIDS-related complex."

7.
"The Book of Wisdom got it right."
"Though he die early—." "He was caught up."
"Before he knew." "—he is at rest."

8.
He led us to the mountain and then he slipped inside.

9.
Switch to the church exterior. Show all
the figures exiting through the paneled doors.
Once children, we would have followed the Piper.
Now we follow the undertaker.

NORWEGIAN SPRUCE

Have you stood next to
a Norwegian spruce and looked up
through the fretwork of swinging
prickly limbs?

I have, and the experience
leads me to boast
about the coarse texture
of the dusty blue branches

that pressed into me like multiple
incisions, until I regretted the loss
of my perfect covering of skin—
what you always admired?—

and realized I was shapeless and bleeding.
You offered me your grandmother's shawl,
your aunt's kimono; still, I was hurting,
and this was no time for theatrics,

even if it was summer and we enter-
tained a troupe from the provinces.
Perennially Phoenician, you would ask,
do Lutherans take communion?

which would become the moment of impasse,
because what difference did it make?
I was at the threshold of knowing
and losing everything to

the swishing, beckoning meditation, and you
wanted to discuss our differences. There was
the moment of exaltation, and—just as
Cindy Crawford responded to the long-haired

journalist who got too personal—
You don't want to know—
I hid what had happened next:
an overture from the African shores

blowing over the fjords
is something like it. Do you mind?
Such is the difficulty of being lovers
in a world where seasons are short:

our Norwegian spruce is an obstacle.
On those days in June when we dare
spend afternoons reclining in the sun,
it looms like an over-protective monument;

we push the mower over grass
and it grabs us by the arms and neck,
a tall, imposing blue-eyed man,
who would take away our pleasure in the end.

ALLIUM

In the garden, I began to lose myself
in the repetition of the deed,

grasping the trowel and pushing it
into the bed of allium bulbs,

the benign kitchen herb of the domestic,
grown gnarled and horrific,

so long ignored they no longer bloomed.
I hurried as I worked, expecting

the arrival of my mother—the quiet click
of the car door, the peal of her anxious voice—

who gardened by the book or expert advice,
whose arrangements formed the table's centerpiece,

a topic of conversation to smooth over
that difficult special occasion.

Would she understand that these were the dusty
nuggets of the ordinary, the overlooked?

Suddenly, millions of bulbs spilled
from the garden's crust like innards

from a dry wound. I reached
with my bare hands to gather them in

and soon filled half a bucket,
soon had enough to fill a field.

I looked up to see my mother standing above me,
wreathed in sunspots, black on red.

COLLECTOR OF GUNS

His was the lot of a family of five women.
We sensed how gingerly he walked
through the well-managed quasi-mansion.
He had to keep his temper in check.

His guns—muskets, pistols, single barrels—
hovered on wooden, hand-made blocks
in his study and above the stairs.
His favorite was an old matchlock.

At the tip of his tongue, a treasure trove
of stories about Buffalo Bill's longest run
as Custer with the Wild West Show
where the Indians always won.

My mother encouraged us,
three girls in ankle socks and Mary Janes,
to challenge the verity of his omnibus.
We danced around him like jumping beans.

He claimed to be hard of hearing
and offered us a businessman's smile,
officious above his military bearing:
that squared, blue-suited guile.

We knew he was concealing something
about his life, but we didn't know what.
"He never tells us anything!"
Mom would say. My aunts would tut tut tut.

We clamored for an unexpurgated version.
Perhaps he kept a secret diary.
Unemployment, war, the Depression!
With his will, an unfinished family tree.

To inspect the contents of the safe,
my mother forced the bolt.
Behind a false wall and cobbled leaf,
she found a loaded Colt.

MATERNAL GRANDPARENTS

In my stringbean adolescence, Granddaddy filled the part
of a tin soldier looking for a heart,

and Mima was the displaced queen, having
dismissed all her attendants and ladies in waiting.

They reigned in the middle of the Pennsylvania German belt,
where they taught, by default, an indifference to wealth.

Each leg of furniture a claw; varnished talons
grasping a mahogany globe, the fierce pride of possession.

Thanksgiving was a tribulation to endure:
cold potatoes, warm soda pop, Mima dizzy with a temperature.

In silent dissent, mother always wore the same dress,
and father immersed his visits in silent rounds of chess.

I was a fledgling of my own design; one minute Ophelia,
the next, a wild child at large in Philadelphia.

How the lines blur between approval and disapproval!
With Granddaddy gone, the neighborhood advanced to the front door,

challenged the years of prestige, and reached for the lock,
like prickly moss absorbing rock.

How I long to go back there!
I'd revamp those domestic dramas from the middle stair,

would seize Granddaddy's forbidden Civil War dagger
and stride to the front door with a swagger

certain that Mima, with her pearls
and her girls' school luxury of never having to act like a girl

would let me cut out a frock from an old drape;
that Granddaddy would help me make my escape

through a passageway hidden by the bookcase in the hall
where a shining future beckoned through the present's murky pall.

WOMAN AT MARKET

She disappeared between narrow rows
of quartered melons and cantaloupes,
unblemished apples and out-of-state cherries,
hard brown pears and prepackaged cranberries,
searching for something she wanted
where the market ceiling was vaunted
and banners of growers were flaunted.

Once a week she slowly surveyed
the produce and groceries arrayed
according to color, size, and function
to ease a buyer's compunction
about purchasing more than her ration.
We saw her again at the counter
where the bleach sits beside fabric softener
in this market provisioned and creedless,
where grapes could be seeded or seedless,
where strawberries fresh or just frozen
might be handpicked and sold by the dozen,
where she chose but never was chosen.

At the funeral home she was laid
in a casket of quality grade
before a floral embankment
that created a seasonal accent.
On her bed of ivory satin
tucked to conform with convention
her face was the color of frost,
her expression one of the lost
who forfeited glory for good
and feared the ring and the wood
as vain assertions of selfhood.

Her son sat and wept in the corner
the most inarticulate mourner,
who barely greeted her daughter—
his sister—who sipped from a bottle of water.
Her husband explained to a neighbor
that he loved but never had known her.

The nurses remembered her last days
when her manner suddenly changed.
She shouted—it was so unlike her!—
that someone was plotting her murder,
and no one could lessen the danger
she faced, a victim of imminent crime.
She described—as if for the first time—
in a narrative clear and undaunted,
how finally she, the tormented,
possessed something somebody wanted.

JACK-IN-THE-PULPIT

Failing farms were sustaining
lives of a few families
and abandoned barns
offered visions of a bygone beauty;
fields once inhabited by cows
had become housing lots
while the church bell tolled.
Watching all this,
my father was dubious.

He returned from the hospital
like a prodigal, uneasy,
exhausted, not sure how to fit in.
Sometimes we heard him laughing
to himself, and sometimes he sat
with us in front of the television;
he liked the series with Ben Gazzara,
who had one year to live.
My father lived six.

Suddenly he began
to record every species of flower
within walking distance.
Mornings and afternoons
he studied the woods,
guide book in hand.
He knelt on the ground
to set the camera on short legs.
One day, he let his glasses slip
off his nose into the brown leaves.

The finished slide shows
the Jack-in-the-Pulpit
as if he had stepped inside,
found his place at the lectern,
and stood looking up
at the striped vegetable cap.

ARMLESS SPRUCE

The southeast tree has lost its arms.
Ripped from their joints and left to dangle,
Branches hang down after storms
Have made deformity the angle
Which must be severed at the joint.
These sticks, now brittle stumps, cannot
Be healed, though salved with healing paint.
They have no use, but waver, fraught
With grief. This heart, by loss defined,
Might swing through empty afternoons
In search of a directive mind,
Like one unmoored among the loons
Who cries aloud for some release
But finds instead a deepset doubt
That only makes its fears increase.
Then winds bring on the winter drought.

The tree I see has raised alarm
About avenging wounds and wrongs.
The tree I know is duly calm;
Songbirds voice its tender songs.
In circles of expanding years,
This tree will thrive in falling rains
And free itself from ancient fears,
Endure the rite of birthing pains
Where sorrows yield to blossoming
And flowers cultivate our trust.
Its passion strengthens from within
Amid eternal restlessness,

Not as some makeshift antidotes
Might balance wrongs with violence.
Once the unarmed alleviates
Its injuries and appetites,
May the tree in my heart express
A love for you, the weaponless.

LINES TO ALLEGRA

You would have liked Jasper Johns
for whom work is a way
to free himself from a bind—
the sticky entrapment of the literal—
in order to move on the surface of things.
What we want is underneath, hidden
and whole, like bubbles not yet broken,
or else it's beyond, gnashing
and roiling out there, full of portent.

Those summers we worked in Provincetown,
we believed that if only we understood
the Tao of Romanos Rizk, the logic behind
Coltrane's *Ascension*, the dreams of gay waiters
on Commercial Street, the remedy
for parents' jealousy of their children,
we would know enough.
These were outside the domain
of the System, which didn't care about us.
On our quest for the Subjective
we carried a deep distrust of all systems,
especially the rigid binary one
that proclaimed divisions where the shadowy
truth could only be found in between.

The idea that somewhere our other half
was wandering in search of a single
perfect mate to complete his body
and soul seemed far-fetched then.
We scorned the theory of one step removed,

and welcomed intimacy and strangeness,
believing that by virtue of proximity with another
our feelings would generate enough electricity
to separate the likes from the loves,
and it would be a simple matter to know
which one to choose: the boy playing
with the ball who was not too young,
not the father's favorite,
not disguised, but apparent
like a precious ring sinking to the bottom
of the pool, glinting there, and bright and lasting.

In a world where love would be so obviously known
we lived as if it were better to wade through
experience without testing the depths,
like soldiers palming hand grenades
before horrified bouquet-bearing civilians.
It was unsettling for me when
we vowed never to marry
and reneged on the promise!
Suddenly it seemed that married and unmarried
were part of the same dichotomy,
no way of knowing what lies underneath
while the flood carries you away.
Why else did Scheherazade depend on her wits
to save her life on her wedding night?
I thought you, for sure, were immune
to that desperation.

You had it made: you,
a painter, married a guy named Art!
Forfeiting ceremony, you embraced
a minimal policy that would defer
to your passion for work.
You had no property, no children, no money.
Then you moved to California where
he decided he wanted what he had been denied,
a conventional wife,
a regular salary, a desk job.

There was no going back,
just sitting quietly and watching
the alternating of this see-saw destiny,
where the occasion for its opposite
would make what is sacrificed now only seem
more attractive later—
you told me, this is it, it's over,
yet I predicted Art would call you when he was
lonely as a father,
encouraged by the new
wall of separation between you.

This wall became a surface
where feelings could emerge.
I can see you with Art
on opposite sides of the table,
your heads of uncontrolled hair nearly touching,
trying but not reaching reconciliation.
Then it is clear that Art is becoming your art:

an afternoon stretching large canvases,
applying the veil of turped-down color—
umber, ochre, venetian red—
to create a middle tone
for the next pastiche of oils,
to give the chastened or roughed-up self
a surface to crest through while protecting
the soul from too much scrutiny.

A Weeping Woman mixes patterns
of short lines at odds like prickly herringbone,
circles with heavy white tears,
two-headed arrows that seek
opposite directions.
The tactile surface of emotions shimmers
like the promise—what you see is what you get—
but underneath all certainty falls away
and the emptiness that is left
is all there is.

As a stone falls, does it think it is going to the ground
because it wants to? (Spinoza)
We have so many new ways of seeing things.
From an orbiting satellite,
we are afforded a new perspective of the earth:
a planet in its infancy
wreathed in watery clouds
that wash over its sphere like expressions
over the face of a sleeping child.
How I long to take care of it,

hold it, nurture it! (It's the mother in me.)
Yet to look beneath the movement of clouds
is to see a multitude of figures like ants
scurrying over the porous skin,
changing habitats, storing food, stealing,
dying, warring with each other, starving
each other out—!

Johns has painted the word "No"
as if it is the pendulum of our protest
years. Frank O'Hara wrote that it is Johns's
business to resist desire. Who would
associate that with the nineteen sixties,
when it seemed desire was the means
and the end?

Or is this the art of courtly irony
now that irony has been promoted
to a full-fledged "feeling,"
neither hot or cold but both and?
The word in gray metal hangs on a gray wire
before a gray ground:
we said no to the war and witnessed a holocaust;
no to the status quo and were often out of work;
no to the denial of sex and watched
the fickle fluctuations of appetite
from one season to the next.
Can one learn from these vacillations?
Am I smart enough?
Perhaps another degree would help!

I would apply for time to figure all this out
(eight years toward a dissertation would be nice!)
but for the example of William Blake,
who found freedom in contradictions
without finishing high school.

The Sixties love of Zen decreed
that to get beyond desire is the only way
to reach internal peace.
The world is too much with us, yet
our longings betray an appetite which
insists the world can never be with us enough.
Or am I confusing world with spirit?
Why has it all become so separated?

Elsewhere, Johns burns paint
into the canvas with wax
and fixes the color with heat,
manipulating the thick surface texture
in the moment's momentum
according to trial and error, intuition,
an old formula, accident, past experience,
all of the above.

In *According to What* Johns gathered tools
to measure the viewer's response:
the painter's scale of primary colors,
photographer's gray card,
Rorschach test; mere representations
until something in our psyche

blooms. It is as if Johns is teasing us
about our need to take stock of things,
to measure what we feel against
the standard, as if he knows how afraid we are
of the raw rind of reality.
He toys with the notion that we can only
accept things by halves—
the brilliancy of light or shadow,
gradations of black or white,
a woman either young or old—
until we can see the thing for what it is,
lines on paper, a design.

And color? Optics explains how when
we gaze at one color, our minds insist on seeing
its complement when we look away,
as if we must automatically experience
despair as part of love
in order to comprehend love.

Lichtenstein's series of the cathedral
at Rouen, the same image
reproduced in varying palettes—
as if weather changes are systematic!—
is a good dig at the labors of Monet,
and Rauschenberg recorded the patterns
of a tire track on a scroll of paper:
create art while you drive.

How is the weather in sunny L.A.?
Are you getting any painting done?

Perhaps you don't like Johns. Who's
your favorite artist now? Are you
perfecting a new skating routine
at the indoor rink in the California desert,
your blades etching clear lines
on the manufactured ice
before it leaches away into the sand;
or studying the sky of the canyon at dusk
with an armful of pastels,
not like a member of an audience
on the edge of her seat,
but like the conductor stage center,
capturing the transforming colors;
and after that the satisfaction
of enjoying the sense of things,
the spontaneity of movement,
the violet of sky, of a loved one,
alone but not alone, knowing
all the while that at Rouen
the light still transforms the cathedral
and in someone's imagined industrialized town
a single rotating tire records the passage
of time on a lengthening asphalt road?

FROM THE LAND OF THE LOTUS EATERS

…[B]ut those who ate this honeyed plant, the Lotos,
never cared to report, nor to return:
they longed to stay forever, browsing on
that native bloom, forgetful of their homeland.

Book 9, The Odyssey,
translated by Robert Fitzgerald

1. The Advantages of Driving

We count kilometers by Peterson's profiles
and petal-falls; just as one toothed frond
disappears quickly into the gaping space
of the right-hand mirror, we look ahead
and identify another, sequential signs
in a revolving gallery, ordered and framed
in the memory. But for these signatures,
we would lose the object of our travels:
to savor the minutiae of distances and hours.

2. Idlers

Lovers who must identify the stars,
we talk about the difference
between loons and cormorants.

Both are black, both dive,
but the latter has a straighter profile,
no white revealed

when it flies, and none
of those eerie, punctuated cries.
You do not want

to believe that the birds rising
up before the prow of our boat
are the same birds

that holler from the woods.
Aren't loons reclusive,
unwilling to be seen

while cormorants are difficult to scare?
Isn't witnessing the ascent of a loon
like discovering a treasure?

We scan the seas for silhouette or code
to relieve the vast expanse
that comes between us,

what we know and cannot know.

3. The Local Boy

The boy who delivered propane
has aged a decade in a year
or forfeited his innocence.

He's wearing flimsy tie-dyed pants.
His smile shows fewer whitened teeth.
To lift our bags he heaves his girth

and no longer shows interest in
our books about species of birds.
He often looks at us askance.

I envy his new competence
manning the boat with ease between
the markers bobbing on the lake

as if he knows all that he needs
to know, the hidden benefit
of learning through experience.

He jumps out on the dock and bends,
revealing skin across his back,
so smooth but for that purple scar.

4. Loosestrife

"The leafy plant, which usually grows about five feet tall, pops up
mostly in areas that have been disturbed."
P.J. Skerrett, *The Boston Globe*, September, 1990.

We drive to this land of vacation
where acres of stubble and standing water

left by the loggers (long ago gone)
have been taken over by a magenta flower,

that compensates for the upheaval
by sealing the lowlands

with a blanket of green stalks sporting purple flames
like banners erected to attract non-natives.

We have read about the voracious
appetite of the water-loving plant,

but now we find the vision inspiring,
look out and admire the blossom's luxuriance,

dream of staying through the winter
in a season of summery bliss,

and we fall in, soon enough, with the Lotos Eaters,
who show no will to do us harm,

who would instruct us on the proper etiquette
for ingesting flowers and forfeiting power.

We forget that we have come here to return home.
At night we dream and forget our dreams.

We become convinced that we are as disturbed as the land,
that to lose strife is to gain everything—

Then the sun's lance and echoes of the meadowlark
remind us of Yeats's land of islands,

and we are brought to our senses.
The dove-grey pages fill with footholds of ink

and we open our minds to know
what the poets surrounded by water know:

that indolence is needed to make music
and amethyst prerequisite for joy.

Notes

"Spruce Down"

The bill from the arborist who cut the dying spruce "down, no clean-up" was fifty dollars.

"Hardgate"

Hardgate is a village in Clydebank, which is a distant suburb of Glasgow, Scotland, where my husband visited his great aunt in 1990.

"Society of Boys"

Claret lemonade is a combination of burgundy wine and lemon juice served to young women, *entre deux guerres,* who did not wish to succumb to intoxication.

"The Rodin Drawing"

More than 7000 drawings were in Rodin's possession when he died in 1917. The most notorious forger of Rodin drawings was Ernst Durig (*Rodin* by Frederic V. Grunfeld, Henry Holt, 1987).

"Uses for Wood"

A definition of "district heat" paraphrased from the *Encyclopedia Britannica*: dating from 1877, the arrangement of piping steam (or hot water) from a single plant to a number of buildings, at first those in the business districts of large cities. The federal government built these plants in the 1930s to serve residential neighborhoods during the Depression. My grandparents' house was located next to such a plant, called a "steam house," in the Germantown section of Philadelphia, Pennsylvania.

"*Near the Beach, Shinnecock,* by William Merritt Chase"

The epigraph is from the journals of William Merritt Chase as quoted in *American Impressionism* by William H. Gerdts, New York: Abbeville Press, 1984.

"*Franklin Park, Boston,* by Maurice Prendergast"

Lines in italics are from Part III of the essay "Painting in Boston, 1870-1930" in the catalogue to the exhibit, *The Bostonians: Painters of an Elegant Age, 1870-1980*, Boston: Museum of Fine Arts, 1986, and from the flyer to the exhibit.

"Brooch"
This poem was inspired by a photograph in *The Boston Globe* that accompanied an article about the Persian Gulf War, 1991.

"There Are Days I Cannot Read"
This poem uses expository lines from Marianne Moore's "The Steeple-Jack."

"Lines to Allegra"
The first stanza is based on commentary about "the bind"—its literal, binary, and precise nature—in Johns's work as described by Max Kozloff (*Jasper Johns*, M. Kozloff, a Harry N. Abrams Book for Meridian Books, World Publishing Company, New York, NY, 1973). He writes that Johns worked on the impulse "to conserve energy and remember what is on the surface." The first lines in stanza 13 refer to the method of encaustic, or burning in, in which the artist applies paint from pigment mixed with melted beeswax and resin, then fixes it with heat.

"From the Land of the Lotus Eaters"
The epigraph is from Book Nine in Homer's *The Odyssey*, translated by Robert Fitzgerald, the Anchor Books edition, Doubleday & Company, Inc., 1963. Lines in italics in the poem "Loosestrife" are also from this translation.

ABOUT THE AUTHOR

Joyce Wilson, editor and creator of *The Poetry Porch*, a magazine on Internet at www.poetryporch.com, has taught English at Suffolk /ersity and Boston University. Her poems have appeared in literary nals such as *Antigonish Review, Agni, Cyphers, Harvard Review*, and *ry Ireland*. One of her poems won the Daniel Varoujan Award from New England Poetry Club of Cambridge, Massachusetts, and another the Katharine Lee Bates Award from the Falmouth Historical Society. reviews books of poetry regularly for *Harvard Review;* other reviews be read online at *The Drunken Boat* (www.thedrunkenboat.com).